FIRE FROM THE HEART
2022

WINNERS OF THE 2022
MURIEL'S JOURNEY POETRY PRIZE

THREE OCEAN PRESS

Library and Archives Canada Cataloguing in Publication

Title: Fire from the heart, 2022 : winners of the 2022 Muriel's Journey Poetry Prize.
Other titles: Winners of the 2022 Muriel's Journey Poetry Prize
Identifiers: Canadiana (print) 20220419353 | Canadiana (ebook) 20220419396 |
    ISBN 9781988915425 (softcover) | ISBN 9781988915432 (EPUB)
Subjects: CSH: Canadian poetry (English)—21st century. | LCGFT: Poetry.
Classification: LCC PS8293.1 .F577 2022 | DDC C811/.608—dc23

Editor: Kyle Hawke
Cover and Book Designer: Kyle Hawke
Cover art: *Freedom to Fly* ©2022 Janet Kvammen

Three Ocean Press
8168 Riel Place
Vancouver, BC, V5S 4B3
778.321.0636
info@threeoceanpress.com
www.threeoceanpress.com

First publication, September 2022

MURIEL'S JOURNEY

The Muriel's Journey Poetry Prize is in its fourth year! It is wonderful that every year, we get to interact with people who knew Muriel. This year we had Gilles Cyrenne as a judge, who knew Muriel well from their interactions in Vancouver's Downtown Eastside.

As we face climate change, threats to democracy, and an ever-mounting crisis with toxic drug supply that has killed more people in British Columbia than COVID-19, I am more grateful than ever to the poets who not only contributed to this edition but also contributed in so many ways to their communities. We cannot face these threats on our own. I know Muriel would have been so proud of all of you!

Many, many thanks to Kyle Hawke, my co-organizer, who also put in the labour of love to edit and publish this chapbook. Equally, thanks go to the judges, Wanda Kewehin-John, Heidi Greco, and Gilles Cyrenne; to Janet Kvammen, who donated the cover art; to Tova Mori, who administered the incoming poems; and to Word Vancouver, who sponsored the award ceremony.

ISABELLA MORI, on the traditional, ancestral, and unceded territory of the Sḵwx̱wú7mesh (Squamish), Səl̓ílwəta?/Selilwitulh (Tsleil-Waututh) and xʷməθkʷəy̓əm (Musqueam) Nations, (Vancouver, BC, Canada)

ABOUT MURIEL AND THE PRIZE

Muriel was a social justice activist, poet, and spoken word artist of Indigenous heritage from the Gitxsan nation's Owl Clan who spent a lot of time in the Downtown Eastside. In her work, she always explored new ways of expressing herself, always talked and wrote about what's urgent and important. Her energy was like fireworks, and her hugs legendary.

Muriel died in November of 2018. At Muriel's memorial at the DTES' Listening Post, someone related that on her last day, Muriel said that while she was leaving, she was still continuing her journey. The text was accompanied by a picture of the sunrise on the day she died. Isabella was moved by this to do her part in Muriel's continued journey and decided to start a poetry prize in Muriel's honour.

Everyone liked Muriel. She encouraged creative people of all stripes to continue on their path of creativity and social justice. With the Muriel's Journey Poetry Prize, we hope to pass on inspiration and strength to all who create with a sense of justice in mind.

Because Muriel always did things a little differently, we're doing this poetry prize adifferently, too. Being keenly aware of how subjective the judging of poetry can be, we give a prize to a poet randomly selected from the longlist of those who met the entry requirement of "lively, outspoken ideas … speak your mind and let the world know what you think … look at your subject in an unexpected way … take a risk in your composition … be frank and unreserved." Another change is our 'entry fee', which consists of people showing how they contribute to their community. Lastly, we have two first prizes, a general one and one specifically for a poet with close ties to the Downtown Eastside.

All poems in this collection were submitted and subsequently were selected by judges as the winners of the second annual Muriel's Journey Poetry Prize.

Prizes were awarded at a ceremony on September 17, 2022 via Zoom as part of the Word Vancouver literary arts festival. The ceremony was hosted from the traditional and unceded territory of the Musqueam, Squamish, and Tsleil-Waututh peoples, but included winners reading from their home territories, as noted in their Community Involvement statements at the end of this book.

ORGANIZERS
Isabella Mori
Kyle Hawke

JUDGES
Wanda John-Kehewin
Gilles Cyrenne
Heidi Greco

Special thanks to the Vancouver Public Library, the Carnegie Centre, and the Heart of the City Festival for allowing us a platform to build on, as well as to Glenn Mori, who worked out the slushing system for the poems. Thanks also to Cecily Nicholson, Diane Wood, and past organizer Rudolf Penner, without whom this whole project would have never happened.

The Muriel's Journey Poetry Prize honours the vitality, vivacity, and outspoken presence of poet-activist Muriel Marjorie, who passed on in the fall of 2018. As an Indigenous social justice activist, poet, and spoken word artist, what Muriel had to say would often literally wake you up. Her enthusiastic encouragement of innovative creative endeavours was infectious.

The Muriel's Journey Poetry Prize is open to all residents of Canada and to Canadians living abroad. No submission fee is charged; instead, those entering are asked to provide a statement of their community involvement to demonstrate their active effort to improve the world around them. First prize is $100. The DTES prize is also $100 and celebrates poets with a deep connection to Vancouver's Downtown Eastside. Second prize is $50. One randomly selected poem will receive $35. Judges look for lively, outspoken texts that present ideas in unexpected ways.

For information on the Muriel's Journey Poetry Prize, please contact the organizers at poetryprize@murielsjourney.com or visit their Facebook page.

www.murielsjourney.com

Contents

A Mourning Aubade (Glosa)
Janet Kvammen

Grey with illness and with age —
a silverpoint against the pillow's white
shone suddenly like the sun
before you died.
 — "Evening Dance of the Grey Flies," P.K. Page

Before you died
I didn't notice their flight
or see their shimmery blue pale
against a golden-ambered dawn.
In the end, did you see them too?
Flitting dancers alit on sky of gilded cage,
their iridescence captures the eye
and we're not alone. It was October then,
its face faded by grief and rage,
grey with illness and with age —

and now years of yesterdays suddenly triggered,
PTSD shudders, flashback horror,
a blood-splattered sink, radioactive daze
and sleepless voids, counting your breaths
while holding mine, words whispered to the dead.
Making it through another night,
the cold house burrowed deep into bone.
We must turn another page,
winter's coming light
a silverpoint against the pillow's white.

Still, we have the happy years
and the lost years.
That last summer, when you came back
for a little while, laughing in the weeds,
we planted seeds of a trip that we both knew
would never come, before the cancer spread,
and madness came undone —
fluttering as wings, a thunder in the chest.
That way you called me 'sweetheart'
at the end. All my hopes outrun,
shone suddenly like the sun.

As once I was a small child,
safe on my mother's lap.
But I was 34, exactly half your age.
A lifetime passed in that golden hour
and a week later, you were gone.
The gospel of Elvis played at your bedside.
You send dragonflies to remind me
of the things I need to believe.
White and blank as pain, even the stars cried
before you died.

Hi Ya, Hi Ya
Brad Akeroyd

"Hi ya, hi ya, thank you, Creator,
for all the good people in this world..."
began the prayer Fred sang and drummed to
each morning in his room at the Pennsylvania.
Fittingly, because Fred Albert Arrance,
longtime resident of the Downtown Eastside
Elder, teacher, brother from another mother,
taught me how to love and respect others.

Born in St. Boniface, Manitoba, Fred,
like his Cree-Métis ancestors, was a survivor.
Age ten ran away to Downtown Vancouver,
spent first night sleeping on the steps of Carnegie.
Ward of Children's Aid eleven to seventeen;
group homes, gangs, graduation from the streets,
learning who to trust and how not to get caught.

Fred lost thirteen members of his family
to substance abuse, violence — on the streets.
Decided to spend his life connecting his people
to the land, spirituality, and culture.
Believed recreational and cultural activities
alternatives to alcohol, drugs, a way to heal.
As a youth activities worker, Fred led groups
canoeing the Bowron Lakes chain,
wading in mud on the West Coast Trail.

Fred's passion was slo-pitch softball.
His team, the Spartans, were stalwarts
of the Downtown Eastside Slo-pitch League.
Fred recruited players walking down the street.
His pitch, "Hey, you look like you play ball!"
Often said, "Down here, there isn't much to entertain,
watching or playing ball is what people love to do."

over

What fired Fred up was the fight for a voice
with the institutions and organizations, stating
"We are recipients rather than participants
in deciding how money meant for us is spent."
Fred formed a non-profit society: WAND
West Coast Aboriginal Network on Disabilities.
WAND worked to raise awareness, money
for cultural activities, always with the motto,
"Do things in a good way, everything will work out."

WAND members used their connections
with other organizations to provide opportunities:
camping trips hosted by the Squamish Nation.
Participants shared traditions, Witnessed first-hand
impact of industry on the Nation's land and water.

In the Downtown Eastside, everywhere evidence
Fred's benevolence, influence on the community.
WAND applied for a $10,000 grant, seed money
for the Memorial Pole in Oppenheimer Park.

Don Larson, Fred, homeless folks in 60 tents
spent 75 days protesting to create Crab Park.
In the park, inscribed on a heart-shaped rock,
Fred's poem, aptly titled *Urban Indian*.
Founding member of Crab Water for Life.
Canada Day, CRAB engages entertainers,
hosts a barbecue: hot dogs and potato salad.
At Christmas, throws a party at RayCam —
Santa gives kids gifts, volunteers serve dinner.

Working at the Aboriginal Front Door Society,
connected with Elders and other Eastsiders.
With family, friends, every Valentine's Day
distributed flowers, food, coffee, water,
for people in the circle at Hastings and Main,
protesting, dealing with loss and pain.

When Fred left us, we gathered to celebrate.
He, dressed in a Spartan jersey, remembered
by loved ones with tributes, drumming,
Women's Warrior and *Going Home* songs.

Now when I hear the cry of eagles circling,
recall a teaching Fred passed on to me:
"Eagles are ancestors watching over us, guiding us,
helping us stay on the Red Road," always.
I thank you, Creator, for Fred, and all the good people.
All My Relations.

Lost Girls

Jacquie Pearce

Last night I dreamed my earlobes were smooth and unmarked by the piercing holes I've had since I was thirteen. I wake to a flash of memory from pre-adolescence — like the wink of sunlight on a drifting spider's thread. There, then gone. I search my reflection in the bathroom mirror for something of that early confidence and sense of possibility — when my imagination pulled toward magic doorways and pirate adventures, and I was better at climbing trees than all the boys. Before everything changed — as with so many young women. Sometimes I imagine her, still there, reaching out for me. The girl before I had scars.

birdsong
there was a language
I used to know

Alchemists Confer with Hypnotists
Dave Olson

Varying days
of bliss and malaise
I'm busy these days
chasing dubbies away

When the ache nears
the break comes and
light becomes a haze
your soul is so faded,
no hiding, so worn

The alchemists confer
and deny the hypnotists'
clinical opinions.
Retorting
"He simply needs
more magnesium
injected directly into his bones"

The past-life regression
of painters and pirates
offered no evidence
only barroom stories when
posted up envisioning
a distant yourself

Generate kinetic watts
from my broken soul,
frantic heart and coiled brain
anxiety — I've plenty to power
all of Iowa — roller rinks and all

Please won't you deplete me
save me from me and help me,
tell me, to sleep? And you'll
insist on my compliance,
fading into ease.

China Creek
Jacquie Pearce

my friend, a single mother,
bought a house
near China Creek Park
— in a city where only decades ago
a woman could not buy a house
without a man co-signing —
her daughter asks
why is it named China
and where is the creek?

> *before the 1900s*
> *60 kilometres of streams*
> *converged at Clark Drive*
> *and East 11th Avenue*
> *fed into Trout Lake*
> *and False Creek inlet,*
> *salmon spawned*
> *boys fished*
> *Chinese immigrants worked small farms*
> *on land leased*
> *from a settler from England*

my friend and her daughter
clear a space for a garden
in their small backyard,
pull weeds
turn soil
prepare it for seeds
imagine carrots, potatoes
bok choi and gai lan

over

the creek
crossed Broadway
flowed north to East 7th
through a deep ravine
became a garbage dump
a bad smell
a health risk
until the City culverted, covered
and almost forgot it

my friend plants tiny carrot seeds
and potato eyes
while her daughter digs
something deeper
first with her hands
dirt under the nails
then a shovel
digging, she says,
all the way
to China Creek

the sound of traffic
from Great Northern Way
almost drowns the memory
of the stream's estuary
and the shores of the inlet
pushed back
and tucked away
for over a century

in the basement
of my friend's house
built in 1916
she unearths the original deed
with the carefully inked words
Must not sell to Orientals

Frosh
Kamila Rina

"...something simple. Each sentence realised or
dreamed jumps like a pulse with history and takes a
side. What I say in any language is told in faultless
knowledge of skin, in drunkenness and weeping"
— "no language is neutral," Dionne Brand

I heard you and those two boys coming down
the dorm hallway from far away. I got a bad feeling
from the volume, the swagger in their voices, and
then a worse feeling as you all paused by my door.
Inside, I held my breath and tiptoed over, looked
through the peephole, saw them intently por-
ing over the pinned-up posters, sniggering, you
standing by, with a confused smug look, then
tipping over into confidence, telling them a stor-
y, something simple. Each sentence realised, or

thrown out thoughtlessly in your eagerness to
please, I couldn't tell. You were discussing my
queerness as if a class of insects: a thing vastly unusual,
bizarre, wholly unconnected to lives you might be
leading, or living beside. My body slowly went cold
as I listened. And then you threw out the hook, a
triumphant sentence: "You know, ze has a thing
for me." My ribs curled in painfully, protectively;
everything I'd barely acknowledged, overlooked as
dreamed, jumped like a pulse with history and took a

frightened gulp of air. Because, yes, I did have a crush
on you. I'd tried so hard to keep it hidden, and there
you were, spilling it to strangers like cheap coffee.
And they hissed delightedly hearing it; you'd just
given them an excuse to let their inner assholes
off the leash. For a moment I still feared assault less
than the humiliation of you knowing this, gossiping
about it — but that changed as they muttered and milled
in front of my door, scraping something on the mess-
age side. *What I say in any language is told with faultless*

precision — carved by years of xenophobic bullying and
my sharp intelligence. This will serve me later when I tell
the story to our floormates, and confront you, all in short
clear words. I had thought we'd understood each other, two
almost-cousins from Eastern Europe, rape survivors, immigrant-
shamed femmes. But after you three leave, and I see the seeping
"I BASH QUEERS" scrawled on my door in purple marker,
I sit down hard, listen to "Jonny and Betty" on repeat, think
of you hugging the toilet last Friday, hug my knees, creeping
with knowledge of skin, drunkenness and weeping.

Sneaking Out
Kamila Rina

We escaped toward the end of September, in broad daylight,
on a plane, clutching tickets we had paid for. We were, it is true, lucky.

We flew on one passport, with a group photo: one dark-haired, firm-nosed
adult, flanked by matching teenager and tween, left ears exposed.

The plane was an old grey Soviet machine, a twin to the one
from the crash in May. There had been no survivors. Not even the plane;

it had dispersed like rain from the burning sky. Damp, still bodies
had been found nestled in the spikes of hawthorn trees.

My mother prayed through all eight hours of the endless afternoon
as we hurtled through time zones. We were still lucky. So lucky.

We brought our belongings. What they had permitted us to take,
what we guessed we'd need, what we could afford

to fit in just three brown and grey suitcases. We left the rest
behind, to cradle someone else's feet now, to fit their lip edge.

We cried over heirlooms needing government permission
for export; getting permits would certainly tip them off.

We saw doctors at night for private appointments,
to secure the required lab work and official medical forms.

We avoided eye contact with everyone else in the dim waiting rooms.
We hoped none of us would give up each other's names.

Though we gossiped quietly, insularly: That family over there? This is
their third round of paperwork. They didn't make it out the other times.

We sold our apartment back to the housing co-op. They rated it
90% Outworn. Which let them keep 90% of our money

while still not needing to renovate it for the tenants buying in.
We liquidated our small savings accounts. We couldn't take cash

out of the country, so we bought some jewellery and a set of fancy dishes
and a fur coat and plane tickets and a hand-woven wool blanket.

We gave away our beloved ugly yellow car, and washing machine.
Even worse, we gave away my beautiful raspberry-coloured shoes.

We could only pack a handful of books, and I agonised
over which printed friends to bring, which to abandon,

never to reunite; our new home did not publish in this language.
I had regrets about *Opium w rosole* and *A w Patafii nie bardzo* for years.

We pretended we were going for a visit, until the last moment,
when we had sponsored visas in hand and our lives in three suitcases.

At that last moment, we said goodbye to friends, coworkers,
classmates, even those whom we hadn't liked very much.

Then we went to be interrogated for hours in the cold belly of the airport.
Saw our belongings rejected and given away for fantastical reasons.

Heard the new dishes smash on the black conveyor belt;
possibly a retaliation for having had so little to steal.

We got on the defective plane, clutched hands, prayed.
To be precise, my mother did; we kids just watched, with anxiety,

the movements of her lips keeping us in the air.
They didn't stop. We didn't stop. We didn't rain down from the sky.

We tiptoed onto someone else's soil (Algonquin nation, I learn later),
fumbling in both official languages. We were so, so lucky.

Activist Anonymous: I've Made Mistakes
Natasha Sanders-Kay

What to do when it doesn't fall under

> Selfish
> Dishonest
> Self-seeking or
> Scared?

>   What if it's something else?

> I've said the wrong things
> Used the wrong pronouns
> Appropriated in rainbow hair extensions and
> Problematic poems

> I fought for an accessible venue but didn't open the door

> Planned a panel during a nervous breakdown
>   Didn't tell speakers that part about no pay

See, I'd rather note I was in crisis than admit
      This was no first-time omission
            Only the first time
                Someone
                  Said
                Something

I volunteered for a controversial women's shelter
            You know the one

And a controversially named march
            You know the one

over

Because of my Politics Power Privilege:

People have felt unsafe in my presence

So have I

Old tools: Scissors Knives Pills Pot

New tools:

Pen Paper

Assurance (not important enough to be cancelled)

Braid glitter pipe cleaner
                    Call it shame Practise touching it

                        chenille squiggles my cats will snatch

~   exhale   ~

Bear my mistakes : Bare my mis-takes

Air my errors

Gather broken glass   Construct a crown

                        Put it on
                        Feel the weight
                            Then lift   it off

Muriel's Journey Poetry Prize 2022 Winners

COMMUNITY INVOLVEMENT

First Prize
Janet Kvammen

From the traditional and unceded territories of the Qayqayt First Nation:
A poet and visual artist who volunteers on the local literary and arts scene, coordinator/host of reading events, writing contests, workshops, art exhibits, and other cultural endeavours.

Second Prize & Honourable Mention
Jacquie Pearce

Jacquie Pearce is a poet and children's book author, living and writing on the unceded territory of the Musqueam, Squamish, and Tsleil-Waututh Nations. In her writing and editing, Jacquie attempts to encourage cross-cultural and environmental awareness, and inclusiveness. Her most recent book for children, *What Animals Want*, is a nonfiction exploration of animal welfare issues (including intersections related to human welfare). Jacquie is a past board member of the Georgia Strait Alliance, is active in supporting haiku poets, and is currently working on a cooperative project to research and translate haiku poems written in Japanese-Canadian internment camps.

Downtown Eastside Prize
Brad Akeroyd

I currently live on the territory of the ancestral and unceded homelands of the Musqueam, Squamish, and Tsleil-Waututh. I contribute by writing about my experiences, current and past, and the people I meet that have influenced my understanding of the community and my heritage as a Canadian of Japanese and European descent. I have been a literacy educator, services worker, volunteer, player/manager of the Oppenheimer Park Pirates, and president of the Downtown Eastside Slo-Pitch League.

Random Selection
Dave Olson

(still) Canadian, now living on generational land in a mostly overlooked corner of provincial Japan with my arborist / jazz singer wife and being an "old dad" to a remarkable toddler with a middle name of Stanley to remind of a park. From a studio in a repurposed storehouse, I endeavour to inspire communities through personal archeology projects, copious correspondence, and fondly supporting friends in foreign lands who have helped me along my healing journey. My creative life archive is at: daveostory.com.

HONOURABLE MENTION
Kamila Rina

Kamila Rina is a multi-disabled immigrant Jewish non-binary poet, educator, and activist. They have been published internationally, including in *Room Magazine*, *Breath & Shadow*, *Carousel*, *Augur*, *The Living Hyphen*, and *Queer Out There*, and produced a chapbook, "Multitasking with Feelings". In their other life, Kamila agitates for tenant rights, radical accessibility, alternatives to policing, and ending rape culture, and leads adult education on consent, gender, disability, and systemic oppression. Born and raised in Eastern Europe, Kamila now lives in Tkaronto/Toronto, located on the traditional lands of the Mississaugas of the Credit, the Haudenosaunee, the Anishnaabe, and the Huron-Wyndat.

HONOURABLE MENTION
Natasha Sanders-Kay

Natasha Sanders-Kay lives and writes on the unceded and ancestral lands of the hənq̓əmin̓əm̓ and Sḵwx̱wú7mesh speaking peoples, including the Hul'qumi'num Treaty Group and šxʷməθkʷəy̓əma?ɬ təməxʷ (Musqueam), Stz'uminus, Qayqayt, S'ólh Téméxw (Stó:lō), and səl̓ilwətaʔɬ təməxʷ (Tsleil-Waututh) First Nations (as far as she knows). She's in her tenth year of volunteering on *subTerrain* magazine's editorial collective, publishing progressive content from a rich variety of emerging writers. Natasha launched the Magazine Association of BC's Inclusiveness in Publishing Initiative, and has also served on the frontlines of causes like land and water protection, stopping demovictions, and supporting womxn and survivors of sexualized violence.

Judges' Statement

The writers explored so many forms — haibun, glosa, prose poems — reading the submissions was a delight. Not only did the poets explore form, but their subjects were just as varied, with topics ranging from childhood memories or beauty in nature to the hardships of city life. Each writer deserves congratulations for putting their thoughts into words and then taking the time to enter.

After reading the works on our own and determining a personal ranking, we gathered for a meeting where we managed to come to consensus (no easy task that, as each of us brought slightly different points of view, but that's likely the reason a jury consists of several people).

We trust that Muriel would look upon these entries with gratitude and pride — after all, she is the inspiration behind the Muriel's Journey Poetry Prize — a journey which we, as jurors entrusted with the challenge of selecting winners, feel honoured to take part in.

WANDA JOHN-KEHEWIN is a Cree writer, originally from Kehewin, Alberta, who moved to BC in 1991. Wanda has been a literary performer and publishing poet since 2011 when she picked up her pen again, which she had put down when she was 16. She has performed her work at many local events.

GILLES CYRENNE lives on the unceded territory of the Musqueam, Squamish, and Tsleil-Waututh people. He has published one book of poetry and is working on a second one. He coordinates the Downtown Eastside Writers Collective and last year was a co-editor of their book, *Continuum*. He serves on the board of the Carnegie Community Centre Association, has worked for the last four years for the Heart of the City Festival, and before COVID, taught a course in English Grammar for the UBC Hum Program, a series of free lectures for DTES people who want to return to academic studies.

Writer and editor HEIDI GRECO's body of work consists mostly of poetry. Her most recent book, *Glorious Birds: A Celebratory Homage to Harold and Maude* (published by Anvil Press in 2021), served as a prose departure in that it celebrates one of her favourite films. While still writing (reviews, blogs, and poems), she continues to dedicate time to matters of environmental protection. She lives on territory of the Semiahmoo First Nation. Find more at heidigreco.ca.